Masterpieces: Artists and Their Works

Leonardo da Vinci

by Barbara Witteman

W
FRANKLIN WATTS
LONDON • SYDNEY

This edition first published in 2004 by

Franklin Watts   Franklin Watts Australia
96 Leonard Street   45-51 Huntley Street
London   Alexandria
EC2A 4XD   NSW 2015

ISBN: 0 7496 5423 6

Series created by Bridgestone Books, published by Capstone Press 151 Good Counsel
Drive, P.O. Box 669, Mankato, Minnesota 56002

Printed in Hong Kong

Consultant: Joan Lingen, Ph.D. Professor of Art History, Clarke College, Iowa, USA

Cover Art: *Virgin and Childwith Saint Anne* (left) and *Self Portrait* (right)

by Leonardo da Vinci

Editorial Credits
Blake Hoena, editor; Heather Kindseth, series designer; Juliette Peters, book designer;
Alta Schaffer, photo researcher; Karen Risch, product planning editor

Photo Credits
Art Resource, NY, 16; Réunion Des Musées Nationaux, cover (left), 20 ; Scala, cover (right),
4, 8 10 (both), 12; Erich Lessing, 6, 18
Corbis/Bettmann, 14

Table of Contents

In *Lady with an Ermine,* shading shows the details of the
weasel's white fur. Leonardo was one of the first painters
to use shadows to make his paintings look more lifelike.

Leonardo da Vinci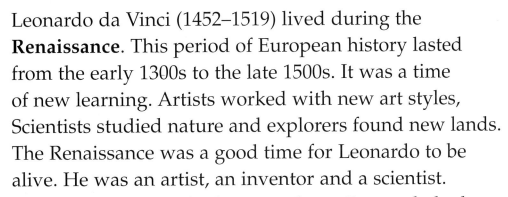

Leonardo da Vinci (1452–1519) lived during the **Renaissance**. This period of European history lasted from the early 1300s to the late 1500s. It was a time of new learning. Artists worked with new art styles, Scientists studied nature and explorers found new lands. The Renaissance was a good time for Leonardo to be alive. He was an artist, an inventor and a scientist.

Even though he had many talents, Leonardo had one big weakness. He left most of his work unfinished. He only completed a few paintings. He often started a painting, got a new idea and then began a new project without finishing what he was working on.

Some of Leonardo's ideas were inventions. He drew pictures of diving suits and weapons. He even hoped to build a flying machine.

Leonardo was also a scientist. He studied the bodies of animals and people. He learned how many parts of the human body work and you can see this knowledge in a lot of his art.

Leonardo painted the angel on the far left in Verrochio's painting *Baptism of Christ*. Apprentices often worked on their teachers' paintings.

Young Leonardo

Leonardo was born in Vinci, Italy, on 15th April 1452. His mother, Caterina, came from a family of poor farmers. His father, Ser Piero, was a rich lawyer. Leonardo's parents did not marry. He grew up with his father's family.

During the 1400s in Italy, children of unmarried parents were not allowed to go to university. Leonardo could neither be a lawyer like his father nor a banker or a doctor. He had to learn a different type of job.

Leonardo liked to draw. Ser Piero showed his son's drawings to Andrea del Verrochio. Verrochio was a famous artist living in Florence, Italy. He liked Leonardo's drawings. In 1466, Leonardo became Verrochio's **apprentice**. Verrochio taught Leonardo to draw, paint, sculpt and design buildings.

In *Adoration of the Magi*, Leonardo made the people and animals look as if they were moving. He was one of the first Renaissance artists to try and show motion in his work.

Adoration of the Magi

Leonardo's skills as a painter earned him work. In 1481, he was hired to paint *Adoration of the Magi* for San Donato at Scopeto, a church that was near Florence. Leonardo's painting shows the three wise men coming to see Jesus Christ.

During Leonardo's lifetime, artists would draw a full-sized **sketch** of the picture they wanted to paint. This drawing was called a cartoon. Artists attached the cartoon to the painting's surface. They then traced the drawing on the surface. Next, artists created the underpainting. They shaded the painting with brown and grey colours. Lastly, artists added the other colours to their work.

It took Leonardo more than a year to finish the cartoon and underpainting for *Adoration of the Magi*. By this time, he was ready to begin a new project and in 1482, Leonardo moved to Milan, Italy to work for the rich Duke Lodovico Sforza. Leonardo left *Adoration of the Magi* unfinished.

Leonardo made many **sketches** of horses while working on the statue of Duke Sforza's father. Leonardo's drawings helped him make a lifelike clay model of a horse.

Leonardo's Horse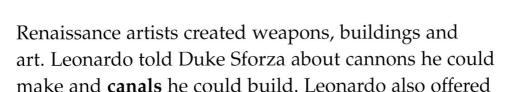

Renaissance artists created weapons, buildings and art. Leonardo told Duke Sforza about cannons he could make and **canals** he could build. Leonardo also offered to make a statue to honour the duke's father.

In 1483, Leonardo began to work on the statue. He wanted to show the duke's father riding a horse. First, Leonardo planned to make the horse. It would stand 7.3 metres tall and would be the world's tallest statue of a horse.

Leonardo took years to plan the statue. By 1493, he finished a full-sized clay model of the horse and then gathered 26 tons of tin and copper. He would make the finished statue with these metals.

Sadly, Leonardo was not able to complete his work. In 1499, the French army attacked Milan. The metal Leonardo had collected was used to make cannon balls and archers shot arrows at the clay horse for target practice.

In the *Last Supper,* Judas (fourth figure from the left) clutches a purse in his right hand. The purse holds the money he was given to betray Jesus (centre).

The Last Supper

In Milan, Leonardo worked on many projects. He began a painting in Santa Maria delle Grazie in 1495. This was the *Last Supper* and he painted it on the dining room wall of this building.

Leonardo painted a dramatic scene in the *Last Supper*. It shows the Apostles' reactions after Jesus Christ tells them that he will be killed. Some of Jesus' followers motion with their hands. Others lean toward Jesus. These actions help show how the Apostles felt about Jesus' news.

Leonardo used **perspective** in the *Last Supper*. This art method was new to Renaissance artists. Perspective shows depth and distance in a painting. In the *Last Supper,* the picture looks as though it goes back into a room.

In Milan, Leonardo also worked on inventions. He made a bright lamp to read by at night. He also built a plumbing system for the duke's castle and designed a diving suit, a helicopter, and a tank. Hundreds of years later, people used his ideas to build these machines.

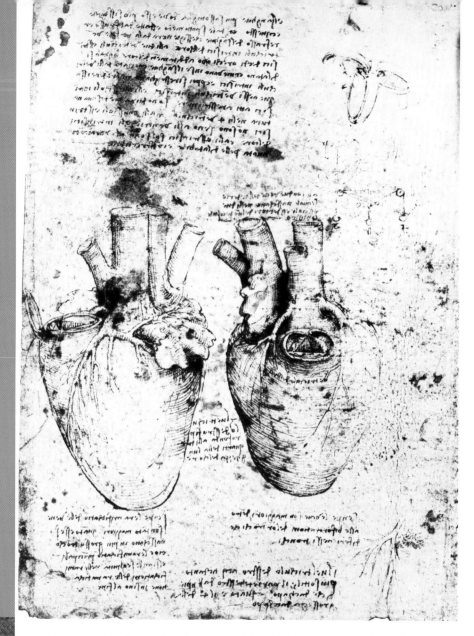

Leonardo drew body parts like the heart, but his drawings were not used by **Renaissance** doctors. They thought people should read books to learn about the body instead of looking at pictures.

Anatomy Studies

Artists often study the human body. They learn about **anatomy** so they can make lifelike paintings and statues of people. During Leonardo's time, artists would go to hospitals or **morgues** to study dead bodies. They cut open the bodies to study their muscles and bones.

Leonardo also wanted to know how the body worked. He cut open bodies and drew sketches of the parts. He learned that nerves begin in the spinal cord. He saw that the heart had **chambers**. He made drawings of the brain and the skeleton.

Leonardo often studied the heart. He made a glass model of the aorta. The aorta carries blood away from the heart. Leonardo attached his model to a cow's heart filled with water. With his model, Leonardo learned that **valves** in the heart open and close and valves control the flow of blood between the heart's chambers.

Leonardo designed a parachute (centre left). He said a person could use it to jump from great heights without getting hurt. He also made notes about his ideas for a flying machine.

Leonardo's Notes

Leonardo had an unusual way of writing. He wrote his notes from right to left. The notes could be read by holding them up to a mirror. Historians think Leonardo wrote this way because he was left handed. Writing from right to left kept his hand from smearing ink as he wrote.

Leonardo wrote more than 5,000 pages of notes. He made notes about his ideas for inventions. He wrote down what he learned about the human body and also took notes about the things he saw while out walking.

Leonardo pasted some of his notes into books. Others were left as he wrote them. Most of his notes have been lost and only about one-third of them have been found. In 1965, two of Leonardo's notebooks were found in a library in Spain.

Today, ten of Leonardo's notebooks are known to exist. They are in museums and libraries in England, Italy, France and Spain. One notebook is in a private collection in the United States.

With *Mona Lisa*, Leonardo achieved something very unusual.
No matter where people stand to look at this painting, they
feel that *Mona Lisa* is staring back at them.

Mona Lisa

In 1506, Leonardo finished his most famous painting, *Mona Lisa*. He tried something new with this painting. He blurred the outlines of objects in the background, making them look unreal. *Mona Lisa* was one of Leonardo's favourite paintings. He kept it with him for the rest of his life.

In 1516, King Francis I of France offered Leonardo a job. Leonardo moved to the king's home in Amboise and served as the First Painter, Architect and Mechanic to the King. Mostly, he and Francis talked about Leonardo's ideas and the things he had learned.

On 2nd May, 1519, Leonardo died. He was 67. Leonardo was buried at the church of Saint Florentine in Amboise. Years later, the church was torn down. Rocks, headstones and coffins from the cemetery were used to rebuild the church. Today, no one knows if Leonardo's bones are actually in the grave marked with his name.

20

Virgin of the Rocks shows the Virgin Mary (centre) introducing John the Baptist (left) to her son, Jesus (bottom right). Leonardo painted it for the church of San Francesco Grande in Milan.

Leonardo's Fame

For nearly 300 years, Leonardo was known only as an artist. But his few finished paintings changed the way people painted. He used shading and showed movement in his art. He also used perspective to show depth in his paintings. These ideas were new to Renaissance artists.

In the 1800s, people began to look at Leonardo's notes. Historians learned that Leonardo's studies were very advanced. His knowledge of the human body and his ideas for inventions showed that he knew more than most scientists of his time. There seemed to be no limit to Leonardo's ideas.

Today, Leonardo is remembered for his art as well as his ideas and studies of the body. His art can be seen in museums in France and Italy. His dreams of flying machines and diving suits have come true.

Timeline

1452 - Leonardo is born in Vinci, Italy on 15th April.

1466 - Andrea del Verrochio makes Leonardo his apprentice.

1470 - Verrochio begins to paint *Baptism of Christ*; Leonardo paints the angel on the far left side of this painting.

1481 - The church of San Donato at Scopeto hires Leonardo to paint *Adoration of the Magi*.

1482 - Leonardo moves to Milan, Italy, to work for Duke Lodovico Sforza.

1483 - Leonardo begins to paint *Lady with an Ermine*.

1489 - Leonardo begins his studies of anatomy.

1492 - Christopher Columbus discovers the Americas.

1495 - Leonardo begins to paint the *Last Supper*.

1499 - The French army captures Milan.

1503 - Leonardo begins to paint *Mona Lisa*.

1506 - Leonardo begins to paint *Virgin of the Rocks*.

1508 - Leonardo begins to paint *Virgin and Child with Saint Anne* (shown on cover).

1516 - King Francis I invites Leonardo to move to France.

1519 - Leonardo dies in Amboise, France, on 2nd May.

Useful Websites

www.mos.org/leonardo
This introduction to Da Vinci separates out the various aspects of Leonardo's genius, and includes sections on his work as a scientist, inventor and artist.

www.ibiblio.org/wm/paint/auth/vinci
This site offers biographical detail as well as lots of fascinating information about paintings.

www.museoscienza.org/english/leonardo/leonardo.html
Really enjoyable site that concentrates on Leonardo the engineer and scientist. Packed full of interactive features including online tours of The Ideal City and a great section on the horse statue and Milan.

www.leonet.it/comuni/vincimus/invinmus.html
Official site of The Leonardo Museum, located in Vinci his home town.

Note to parents and teachers
Every effort has been made by the Publishers to ensure that these websites are suitable for children; that they are of the highest educational value, and that they contain no inappropriate or offensive material. However, because of the nature of the Internet, it is impossible to guarantee that the contents of these sites will not be altered. We strongly advise that Internet access is supervised by a responsible adult.

23

Glossary

anatomy - the study of the human body

Apostle - one of Jesus Christ's 12 followers

apprentice - someone who learns a trade or craft by working with a skilled person

architect - a person who designs buildings

canal - channels of water used for transporting goods

cartoon - Lifesize sketch of painting which artists would trace on to the canvas before adding the paint

chamber - a space in the heart that holds blood

morgue - a place where dead bodies are kept

perspective - depth in a painting; perspective shows distant objects being smaller than nearer ones.

Renaissance - a time of new art and learning

sketch - a rough drawing

valve - a movable part that controls the flow of liquid

Index